SOMETHING BETTER THAN SILENCE

by
Kathleen Fortun

RB
Rossendale Books

Published by Lulu Enterprises Inc.
3101 Hillsborough Street
Suite 210
Raleigh, NC 27607-5436
United States of America

Published in paperback 2016
Category: Life Story/Memoirs
Copyright Kathleen Fortun © 2016
ISBN : 978-1-326-65427-6

All rights reserved, Copyright under Berne Copyright Convention and Pan American Convention. No part of this book may be reproduced, stored in a retrieval system, or transmitted in any form or by any means, electronic, mechanical, photocopying, recording or otherwise, without prior permission of the author. The author's moral rights have been asserted.

Image Permissions & Copyright

Cover image © www.flickr.com: weir on the River Wharfe at Boston Spa

Images on pages 128 and 129 by kind permission of The Cochlear Corporation http://www.cochlear.com.

Image on page 130 by kind permission of The University of Southampton Auditory Implant Services.

Contents

Foreword 7

Early Days 10

The Onset of Deafness 16

Living Away From Home 21

My Life at St John's 49

Life After St John's 87

Marriage 94

My Working Life 97

Brandy 112

My Cochlear Implant 127

Dedication

To The University of Southampton
Auditory Implant Services

Acknowledgements

This story is in no way to disparage the present "St John's" but told as the writer experienced it of her time there in the 50's when it was an Institution. Boarding schools in the 50's were certainly a lot harsher than they are today.

With thanks to Kevin Fitzgerald (author of Deafness of the Mind) for his support in writing my book as without it I would never have made it.

Special thanks to Joselyn Taylor an ex pupil of St John's for providing me with the photographs of St John's.

Foreword

A snail shell. A blade of marram grass. Although these might otherwise be seen as insignificant objects in the hustle and bustle of everyday life, they were in fact the turning point that led to an Australian surgeon developing a pioneering technique to help deaf people to hear.

The cochlear of the inner ear is a bony, fluid-filled structure shaped like a snail shell. The sensation of hearing begins when sound waves reach the eardrum and the energy of these waves cause it to vibrate. This vibration is transferred to the tiny bones of the middle ear: the hammer, anvil and stirrup. This last bone, the stirrup, transfers the sound energy to the fluid in the cochlea by setting it in motion and causing a wave to be propagated along the inside of the cochlea itself. As the wave moves, it disturbs the thousands of tiny hair cells that are situated along the cochlea duct; these hair cells relay information about sounds to the brain via the acoustic nerve. Finally, the brain interprets this information through a complex series of recognition and discrimination efforts which, in a normal hearing person, have typically been developed by hearing experiences from very early childhood.

In severe cases of deafness, sometimes called sensorineural deafness, the hearing loss is a result of the hair cells in the cochlea having become damaged or destroyed. In such cases, even the most powerful hearing aids are often ineffective, although the acoustic nerve itself is, more often than not, intact.

Here the snail shell, the blade of grass, and the Australian surgeon come in. The surgeon in question, Professor Graeme Clark, working in the Department of Otolaryngology at the University of Melbourne was wrestling with the problem of how to bypass the damaged hair cells in the cochlea and stimulate the acoustic nerve. Sitting on a windswept beach, he was attracted to a snail shell which reminded him of the cochlea and, as he turned it over and over in his hands, the idea came to him. Plucking a blade of marram grass he pushed it inside the shell as far as it would go right to the apex of the shell. At this moment, he knew he had a solution to his problem; the grass was an imaginary bundle of electrodes on a fine wire. This moment of inspiration was the spark that drove this remarkable man to develop a prototype implantable device which, in its ultimate form, is now the most widely used cochlear implant in the world.

Early Days

Waking up in my hospital bed at the Royal Hospital for Sick Children, St Michael's Hill, Bristol I remember being confused as to where I was, everywhere I turned to look was strange and silent. I began to cry and a nurse came up to my bed and I remember a doctor soon followed. I had been in what seemed a long coma possibly from my illness and the drugs administered and had woken up. I was eight years old so I didn't quite understand what was happening to me only that I could not hear. I was flown over to Bristol two months earlier in December 1950 from my home in Jersey, Channel Islands by an ambulance plane accompanied by a nurse and my father as I was very ill with T.B. Meningitis. I had been in the General Hospital in Jersey since October 1950 and they could do nothing for me and I was given the last rites by our Parish Priest. By a stroke of luck they then had heard of a new drug, Streptomycin, that was being administered to children in Bristol and if I was to survive my illness then that was my only chance. Now it was January and that month was almost out I was on my way to making a recovery. I was sat up in bed and given something to eat. I remember it was Sunday morning and every Sunday up to the time I was discharged from hospital a man with an accordion used to come and sing to the children in the ward and they all joined in. My mind cast back to the time I was at primary school and how I used to hear the church bells, the hymns sung at Mass and at assembly at school. Now I was plunged into a world of silence. I loved listening to 'Children's Hour' on the radio and now it was just a silent box.

***

My father was a Jersey man and lived on Jersey in the Channel Islands. When he was 16 and war had broken out his parents evacuated from the island taking with them their two sons which were my father and his 14 year old brother. The Germans were coming to invade Jersey and my Grandmother being an Irish woman from Dublin would have been deported to one of their concentration camps in Germany. Only Jersey born people could stay on the Island. For that reason my Grandfather took his family and boarded the last boat to the mainland before the Germans came and fled up to the north of England. As far as I know many people from Jersey were on that boat that day and it was full. Many families arriving in Weymouth took the trains to the north of England to towns like Burnley, Bury, Oldham and Rochdale. My fathers family settled in Rochdale. My Father was 17 when he met my mother and they married when they were 18 and my brother was born in 1941. I soon followed in 1942. When the war ended in 1945 all the family planned to return home so we all came back to the Island in 1946 when I was four years old.

***

I had a very happy childhood up to the time I went deaf, living at home with my parents and two brothers. I went to Val Plaisant School when I was six with my eldest brother who was a year older than me and I loved it there. My teacher Miss Young was wonderful so were the other teachers and I had made many friends. My teachers always regarded me as a very happy little girl who was very attached to her older brother. Getting up in the morning and going to school and coming home again after a long day with a new book to read at bedtime were indeed a very exciting and interesting part of our young lives. The war had ended three years earlier when my brother and I had started school. We had a new baby brother around that time so we were feeling a little grown up and protective towards him. Everything was still rationed in the shops and everyone were making their best efforts to rebuild their lives after the Germans surrendered and had left so much destruction to the island.

Kathleen aged 7 and brother Michael aged 8 in a school play "The Three Wishes" 1949 We are in the middle of the photo (me in pigtails)

Kathleen aged 8 at the Royal Hospital for Sick Children, St Michaels Hill, Bristol. The lady in the photo was a neighbour living next door to us in Jersey, she moved to Bristol so used to come and see me on behalf of my parents.

My parents and my two brothers Michael aged 13 and Bernard aged 6.

The Onset of Deafness

I remember the day when I was eight I collapsed in the playground. It was pouring down that we had to spend playtime inside and the teachers were gathering us in twos to run to the toilets which were opposite the school building. When my turn came to run with another girl the heavens opened and it was thundering. I thought God was very angry as us children used to say. Running half way I collapsed on the tarmac, I remember the teachers picking me up and taking me back into the classroom. They called for my mother, we did not live far away from the school, she came to pick me up with a pushchair as I was very poorly and too weak to walk. Little did I know I would never return to that school again or see my teachers or my school friends. My life was about to change forever.

**

The doctor said I just had a bad cold when he visited me at home that day I had collapsed but I was very weak and could not get up to walk unaided. I was suffering most dreadful pains in my head which were as the doctor said just normal headaches. I remained at home in bed for a couple of weeks and I remember a teacher came in the mornings to give me some education, either reading a book to me or doing simple sums and writing as I was too ill to go to school. My condition deteriorated that my mother called an ambulance and I was taken to hospital. After what seemed like numerous tests they found I had T.B. Meningitis. I was put in an isolated ward, named Robin Ward. I remember my parents used to come and visit and I could only see them through a glass partition. I made no improvement in the coming weeks, and as well as being given the last rites I was confirmed by our parish priest as they thought there was no hope. I remember the times I was put to sleep with chloroform for the purpose of lumbar punctures to draw fluid out of my spine for the laboratory tests. I remember having them throughout my teenage years without any sedation at the beginning of every school year when I used to go to Bristol Royal Hospital for sick children on my way to school, stopping overnight as it was a way of making sure I was clear of T.B. Meningitis. They were not done without a struggle with the doctor administering it, I gave them quite a hard time and the nurses had to hold me down. I hated them that it was a relief to be told on my 16th birthday I no longer had to go to Bristol to have them.

***

During my recovery from my illness I had to learn to walk all over again. My legs were very weak and I lost the ability to walk and lost my balance. I remember the nurses getting me out of bed at certain times of the day to crawl around the wards and as the weeks passed my legs gradually became stronger and I was able to stand and take short steps. I came back home in the Spring of 1951. A social worker from the hospital in Bristol accompanied me home to

Jersey, my parents and grandparents were there to meet me at the Airport. We boarded a coach to St Helier and we stopped at The General Hospital first and memories came flooding back, it had been 7 long months since I left there to go to Bristol. It seemed that the social worker handed notes to the hospital on my care and obviously discussed concerns about what was going to happen to me now that I was deaf. I remember Mr Denny, the ENT Consultant then, putting me on his lap and that I was very afraid of his white coat thinking of all the times a doctor wearing one had put a cloth of chloroform over my face to put me to sleep and I thought he was going to do that. Instead he banged a metal bar with two prongs and tapped them on the desk and put them to my ears to see if I could hear anything. I could not so after some more tests he confirmed I was profoundly deaf. I was still wondering why I could not hear. I could no longer hear my brothers or my parents talk and many of the school friends I made at school who lived in the same street as I did just stopped being friends. Many years later I learned that they must have felt shy and uncomfortable and did not know how to talk to me. My brother with whom I was very close felt the same. My little brother was two then so too young to understand. My parents struggled to make conversation but I was learning to lip read them real fast. My parents used to make me face them and read their lips with exaggerated mouth movements. It just wasn't the same anymore and I knew I was different but I didn't understand at the time what being deaf meant and that I would never hear again.

Living Away From Home

In September 1951 just before my ninth birthday my mother said I was going back to hospital for tests. Nothing more was said. My father took me and we went on the boat to Weymouth and there caught the train to Bristol. When we reached the hospital I was shown into the ward and my bed, nothing much changed from when I was there last except the children I had remembered had all gone home and new ones were in the ward. My father said goodbye and I thought he was coming back the next day to take me home but how wrong I was. The next day after tests a social worker, the same one that had taken me home to Jersey that Spring, came to collect me, said nothing, held my hand and picked up my small suitcase which was some clothes and belongings. I remember she was a kind woman but did not talk to me at all. We went to Bristol Temple Meads Station and from there caught a train to

Leeds. It was a long journey but nevertheless interesting as I didn't remember travelling on a train before, in Jersey there were no trains. When we reached Leeds we went to Vicar Lane Bus Station and caught the bus to Boston Spa which was 14 miles away.

I had no idea where I was going. I just didn't ask. Nobody seemed to explain what was happening to me. I was told that after I went deaf I stopped talking unless spoken to, maybe because I could no longer hear my own voice and that of others. I remember looking out of the bus and seeing all the green countryside, it was vast unlike the fields in the small island of Jersey, the cows in the field I noticed were black and white when in Jersey the cows were brown. In Jersey I lived with my family in the city of St Helier and did not go out into the country so had never seen anything like it. Everywhere was so fresh and green with trees and grass. We lived near the sea and often went to play on the beach at week-ends with my parents and brothers so this was different.

St John's is situated in Boston Spa, Yorkshire, a sleepy village in the heart of the countryside. The river Wharfe runs through it and it is not far from Wetherby and other small villages and towns in Yorkshire. St John's owned several fields and farmland, a cemetery, a farmhouse as well as the huge stone building which housed a chapel, the boys building was on the left of the chapel and the girls building on the right. In between the chapel and the girls building were the sisters quarters. The classrooms were situated on the ground floor of the boys and girls buildings and on the first floors were the dormitories. The three to four year old boys and girls were integrated with the 6 year old girls but they slept in a large dormitory in the sisters quarters until a few years later had their own nursery building built at the back of the girls building. The Principal of St John's lived in a detached four bedroomed house on the side of the school with its own private entrance. In that building were the offices too.

An aerial view of the Institution. You can see in the picture that the boys & girls buildings were strictly segregated by rows of little cottages in the middle of picture forming a courtyard for each of the boys & girls and almost attached to the girls building is the Nursery on the left of the picture for 3 to 5 years olds where Laurence was as told in my story.

St John's Institution for the Deaf & Dumb. On the left of the photo almost hidden is the boys building, the chapel, the Sisters quarters and far right is the girls building.

The cemetery and graves where the children who died young were buried.

Some of the boys and girls who died young wanted to be buried in the cemetery at St John's as it was the only place where they had friends. I remember at least two funerals where we had to form a guard of honour when the coffin was brought in to the parlour. The only people that were their 'family' were the Sisters and children of St John's. Mass was said for them in the chapel and the coffin was moved to the cemetery for burial. We did not go to the little churchyard only the Sisters did. We did not quite fully understand about death at the time but later when I was a teenager we thought it was very sad.

I was two weeks away from celebrating my ninth birthday with pigtails and ribbons that many people thought I looked like Mandy in the Mandy Miller Story. This film was about a little girl who was deaf and how her parents, shocked and upset that she was deaf, tried to find a local deaf school for her. This wasn't in my case however. The authorities thought they were doing the right thing sending me away. I wonder today if any of them at the Education Department had ever visited St John's or even read the reports on it. My parents were never asked to visit St John's, the school they were sending their daughter to. The Education Department in Jersey were paying for my education at St John's as my parents couldn't afford to send me away to a special school, boarding schools were expensive and I do wonder if they knew it wasn't a school but an

Institution. My parents were told it was a good school, my speech would deteriorate if I did not go to a special school for the deaf but little did they know it was a very different world behind closed doors from the one they thought I was entering.

The social worker and I, after alighting the bus, waited for the bus to pass us and there on the opposite side in front of us was a huge stone building. Crossing the road and walking past a rather demeaning sign at the entrance which read:

ST JOHN'S INSTITUTION

FOR THE DEAF AND DUMB

I was too young to understand exactly what those words meant. I did think I was going to another hospital as The Royal Hospital for sick children in Bristol had an imposing stone frontage to it. We went up the steps to a large wooden door. After ringing the bell we were greeted by a middle aged woman clad in grey clothes and who invited us in. I remember the shiny wooden floor that was polished like glass, the copper planters holding plants that looked like palms trees. I later learned that the older girls did all the cleaning and polished the wooden floors daily. In another room we were shown into and which I later learnt was the parlour there were dark velvet curtains, and huge religious pictures on the walls and that of previous Mother Superiors of St John's. It was very dark and eerie indeed. There was a dark mahogany table and six chairs and underneath was a large thick rug of oriental design that covered most of the wooden floor, a huge dresser on one side and a fireplace where the fire was burning. A large mirror adorned the fireplace. We sat and waited and then Sister Barbara entered the room. I gave one look at her and began to cry, the social worker tried to console me. I was afraid of the doctors white coats in hospital and what they may do to me but I had never seen anything like this. The Sisters of Charity were of the order of St Vincent de Paul and wore long navy dresses that seemed to be padded with petticoats, with a starched white bib folded at the front and their head dress were starched white cornets that came out at the side like seagulls wings. There were many seagulls flying around in Jersey as I had remembered seeing them many times when we went down to play on the beach. It made the Sisters look very big indeed and for a small child that can be frightening. Another Sister came in with a silver tray holding a silver teapot, milk and sugar and some sandwiches. I guess knowing how far we had travelled I suppose it was polite to offer us that. I can't remember eating the sandwiches or drinking the tea, my eyes were focused on Sister Barbara's habit that looked so strange. There hung from her waist was a huge wooden rosary with its huge crucifix hanging down one side of her dress and a bunch of keys dangling from her waist on the other side. The social worker had a long talk with Sister Barbara and then came and kissed me goodbye. I clung to her skirt, I was crying hysterically, I just did not want her to leave me there. Sister Barbara calmed me down as the social worker left and took my hand, picked up my suitcase and led me into the workroom and going through the grim corridors it was a very different story to the parlour that was warm and lavishly furnished.

In the workroom I was allocated a locker with a number G4. G as for girls and 4 was my number. This was where my suitcase and my clothes my mother had packed for me was to be stored and was never seen from one term to the next. I had to undress and put on this horrible itchy jumper in navy blue and a dark green gymslip, even my pretty vest, bodice and knickers were taken off and stored in my case. In the summer we all wore short sleeved cotton dresses with white collars that were handed down from previous pupils at St John's. I was given a pair of navy knickers to put on that were too big for me that I was constantly pulling them up. Then one of the Sisters in the workroom came and undid my ribbons and cut off my pigtails. I was then taken to the playroom to meet the other girls. I noticed we all seemed to have the same hairstyle, short and on one side a parting, the other side held back with a hair grip. Long hair was considered vain and a fringe was considered very common by the Sisters I had learnt. I was bewildered and frightened of my surroundings, the sight of the playroom which was bare and had a high ceiling wasn't very welcoming with wooden floor and bare windows that were high above on the walls that we couldn't see outside, there were no curtains just bare windows. There wasn't a picture in sight just a crucifix on the wall. There were about 60 girls whose ages ranged from 6 to 16, who were signing, moving their hands and arms about and it was very frightening. My immediate thoughts must have been that my parents had put me in a mental institution.

That night in a large dormitory, named 'St Joseph' which consisted of twenty iron beds, plain stone walls painted white, bare wooden floors, curtains that were never drawn on the windows and for girls aged nine to eleven I had put on my nightdress and climbed in between the sheets, the beds reminded me of the beds in hospital and only one blanket. I was sobbing between the sheets, I had wanted the social worker to come back and take me home to where I belonged, but knew it wasn't going to happen. At home if I had fallen or been upset my mother would come and comfort me or my elder brother too would put his arms around me but now I was afraid and all alone. There were many visits to my bedside that night from a Sister in charge of the dormitory who I think was Sister Philomena telling me to be quite as I would wake the other children up. The children were deaf so how could I possibly wake them up. The sisters had a rota of sleeping in a cubicle in the corner of the dormitory. It had a door and a little window where they could look out to see if we were asleep or even walking about the dormitory. The world I had known had disintegrated in just a matter of a few hours since stepping inside St John's. Tomorrow I would begin a journey into the deaf world and the Institution and I was trying to imagine how I could live in this place but I was so tired from crying and travelling all that day that I soon drifted off to sleep.

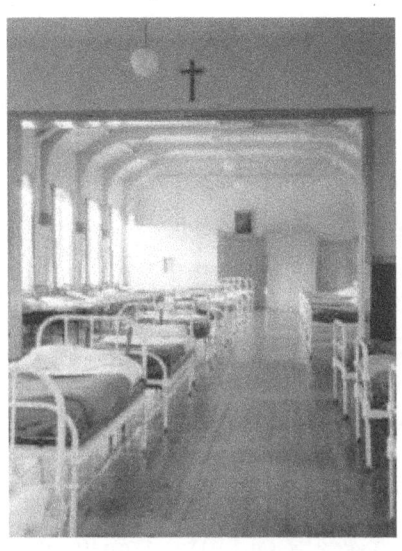

St Joseph's dormitory in 1951 when I entered St John's My bed was on the left, fourth row from the little cubicle with the window for the sisters to check on us.

The door in the background lead to the Infirmary where if you were sick you were segregated in that room.

I was woken early the next morning by a Sister stripping the bedcovers back. We had to get out of bed, kneel and say prayers, then queue up for the washrooms and splash out faces with cold water. This routine was done everyday until I left St John's. I soon learned the water was freezing in the winter. I never remember using hot water only for our weekly bath. Some of the poorer girls did not have any soap or toothpaste so I used to share mine. I felt very sorry for these girls many whom had been there since they were four years old. We made our beds and got dressed. We were taught to pull our sheets tight and tuck corners, it had to be perfectly made for the Sisters to inspect. We descended a large wooden staircase that was polished and which led to the refectory on the right at the bottom of the stairs. As we took the last step down there was a large wooden door in front that lead to a large hall and the classrooms. The corridors as I remember were dark and wood panelled. In the refectory were long wooden tables to accommodate eight girls, years later that changed to proper dining tables for six girls. In this Institution we were incarcerated there from one term to the next. Now I know why the sisters carried huge bunches of keys around with them dangling from their waists. I thought I had done something terribly wrong to be placed there and my only crime was that I went deaf.

I remember the first day in the classroom, it was so different to the classroom at primary school I had attended in Jersey. The children were too small to look out of the window as they were high up. I spent the whole day crying much to the annoyance of the Sister who apparently had shaken me to make me stop crying but she didn't succeed as it made me cry even more. I remember my teacher Miss Young was always smiling when we arrived at school and wore normal clothes but the Sister was dressed in a habit that was somehow foreign to me and I couldn't think where people like that had come from. Her name was Sister Philomena and she was quite a large Sister and I only ever remember her being there for two terms. The Sister had a solemn look on her face and never smiled. I guess it was a habit of hers to behave like that as she may have spent most of her life there. I remember there were two lay teachers but unfortunately I was in the class with a Sister. I remember the last day at primary school in Jersey we made animals out of raffia, winding it around cardboard animal shapes, but in this class we just copied things from the blackboard on paper. It was a dark room and I remember looking at the window which was high up and seeing the sky and trees outside and wondering if I was going to go outside at playtime which we did in primary school but it never happened that day nor in the future. St John's seemed to be very poor on materials in the classroom in those days.

From left to right : Sister Margaret, Sister Teresa, Sister Louise, Sister Kevin and Sister Barbara.

We mostly wrote on the blackboard instead of having an exercise book and pen and a reading book.

This was the sewing and knitting class. Although the photo was taken in the late 1940's nothing had changed when I entered St John's in 1951.

The weeks that followed I settled down, made some friends, it was hard getting used to as it was not like getting up in the morning and going outside to school with my brother, even going home from school. I was thinking of home a lot and pictured my brother walking to school on his own. I loved my brother dearly, we had been inseparable since I was born and there were only 14 months between us. I missed my parents too and my little brother. I felt so far away from home. I was homesick, depressed and subdued for a very long time. Gone were the days when we went out to play in the street at week-ends and knocked on doors or shouted for our friends to come out and play. Here at St John's it was as if I was locked up in an approved school. I soon learnt how to communicate with the other girls learning to finger spell, almost all the girls could not talk and very few could lip read. Many of the girls had been there since they were four so knew nothing else. They began their life in a deaf world whereas I did not. I just couldn't wait to get out of the place and often thought about when that would happen.

St John's Catholic School for the Deaf was founded by Monsignor de Haerne, an influential Belgian priest and senator, in a small house in Handsworth in 1870 with the help from the Daughters of Charity of St Vincent de Paul. The School was relocated to Boston Spa in 1875. Belgian sign language was first taught at the School. From research, in 1880 in Milan it was decided to convert to oralism, to sack deaf teachers of the deaf and replace them with hearing teachers. This had a profound effect on deaf children. As a result thousands of deaf children were turning out illiterate. Many of the children came from deaf families so signing was their only means of communication. However when I was at St John's the Sisters had no objection to signing outside the classroom. In my later years at St John's I used to wonder how these children could learn anything in lessons if they were profoundly deaf and unable to lip read. I do know that many of these girls left school unable to read or write. At first communication either by signing or lip-reading was very difficult so I forced myself to become an excellent lip reader in order to survive life there so I could lip read the Sisters in the classroom and out. Today British Sign Language (BSL) is very different to the sign language at St John's.

For the first few years I remember the lessons were so easy as I had learned very similar at primary school. These lessons were always the same that I did not feel I was learning anything. We wrote more on the blackboard than actually writing in an exercise book. We had no books in the classroom only one book the Sister had and was shared around. There was no library to find any books to read. I have a vivid memory even today about the time I asked Sister Barbara "where are the books". I remembered in primary school in Jersey we were told about black children in other countries who went to school and had no books and the teachers used to say that we must look after our books as children in other countries do not have the privilege of reading books as we do. Well, Sister Teresa from the boys side who happened to come into the classroom at the time giving some advice on teaching looked at me in astonishment and turned to Sister Barbara saying "what books - the children cannot read!" At that point I was just told there were no books. I missed my primary school and the books we took home to read at night and returned the next day for a new one, the exciting things I learned all became a distant memory. It became so boring and school was no longer interesting. In my middle years at St John's we did a lot of practical lessons such as knitting, sewing and cookery. I got the impression that deaf people were only taught to be good with their hands. Reading, writing and using your brain did not seem to exist in a deaf persons education until Canon Kelly came and changed all that.

We went home for the school holidays which were six weeks in the summer, three weeks at Christmas and two weeks at Easter. My father used to meet me in Bristol. He also used to take me as far as Bristol where I met up with the other children for our journey to school. Sometimes if I took a flight from Jersey to Leeds Canon Kelly used to pick me up.

We went out for walks on a Sunday afternoon, weather permitting. We would form a long queue up in twos with one sister at the front, one in the middle and two at the back. Villagers passing used to look at us with pity as if we were orphans and the men raised their hats to the Sisters. No one knew what went on inside St John's. We had to smile and put on a happy front. It was only short walks around the village but at least we were out of that dreadful place. Later on the walks got longer and we were benefitting from the country fresh air. Once a group of us walked to Bluebell Wood which was quite a way away and had a wonderful time picking bluebells and running around in freedom. We couldn't control out excitement to be out in the wonderful woods. Sister Martha who took us couldn't gather us all together to get back on time as many went too far off in the woods. I remember when we arrived back Sister Martha was told off by Mother Superior for getting us back late, at least Sister Martha didn't lose any of us.

Later when I had been at St John's for three years I went home to my Grandmother in Lancashire for two weeks at Easter and for one week-end each term. I always looked forward to going to my Grandmothers house in Rochdale. The journey was by coach over the Yorkshire Dales where you could see sheep everywhere and the tall chimneys of the mills in Lancashire too. In those days I remember the textile mills right across the road from my Grandmother's house which have long since passed away. The family on my mother's side all worked in those mills. Also the coal mines where my great grandfather had worked in Golborne Colliery. Lancashire seemed a very foggy place in those days of tall chimneys and every home seemed to have a coal fire, indeed my grandmother always seemed to have a coal fire burning on my week-ends there in the winter, from the time I got up to the time I went to bed. I was always sad to go back to St John's after my weekend with my Grandmother. The short time even one weekend a term gave me a sense of normality and a break from the walls of St John's.

In winter Lancashire was knee deep in snow as I had found on my visits to my Grandmother. Indeed it snowed heavily in Yorkshire too and at St John's we used to see it snowing from the windows in the playroom though couldn't see the ground as the windows were too high up. It was usually freezing in the room where there was one little fire for such a large playroom. At my Grandmothers the children played in the streets using car tyres and old boxes for a sledge, even throwing snowballs and making a huge snowman. It was sad to think the children at St John's were incarcerated and did not have the freedom to go outside and play.

In 1952 Canon Kelly came to St John's to become the new Principal. Mother Superior was replaced. Two lay teachers had joined the school. I was sorry for the boys side of the school, I heard the sisters were giving them a very hard time. Sister Margaret and Sister Teresa were over on the boys side and were very strict. No doubt they were worn out from using up all their energy punishing the boys for whatever little misdemeanour as they always seemed to have flushed faces. Although the Sisters on the girls side were strict I thought us girls were very lucky to have Sister Barbara.

Over the next five years things gradually began to change at St John's. The first thing Canon Kelly did was change the name of St John's from "St John's Institution for the Deaf & Dumb" to "St John's Catholic School for the Deaf". I do know that Sister Barbara who came to the school in 1950 did not agree with the way us deaf children were treated and I am sure she knew what they were doing was wrong. She was a very young Sister in those days and many of her superiors were a lot older and had been at St John's for a number of years before her. She was a 'teacher' whereas a lot of the Sisters did not seem to be trained teachers. The older sisters had that Dickensian era imprinted on their minds and that is the way of life they treated us children both on the boys side and the girls. I will admit here that Sister Barbara did have her favourites and unfortunately I was not one of them.

Many things came too late for me as when I visited St John's in the 60's many Sisters had been replaced with lay teachers and indeed today there are no Sisters at St John's. Children are getting a better education. Today the whole school, and the education of the deaf, has changed beyond recognition. Children are going on to higher education even University which didn't happen in my day sadly. Even the boarders have more freedom and go home at week-ends and they are involved in lots of outside activities against other schools in the area. Boys and girls are integrated too. I hope another deaf child will never have to go through what I did at St John's.

Then as part of the changes at St John's that were on going many of the older Sisters that left were replaced with lay teachers. None of these teachers could sign very well so it must have been very difficult for some deaf children to learn anything. We were able to sign outside the classroom to other deaf girls but signing was banned in the classroom. We had to lip read. It was great to have lay teachers coming in though, they usually talked to us about what was happening in the outside world. Most of the teaching in the classroom was practical work like knitting, sewing, embroidery and cookery in my first few years there but it soon changed when Canon Kelly came and we were doing more written work, writing compositions and reading books.

*Canon Kelly later
to become Monsignor Kelly.*

My Life at St John's

In all the eight years at St John's, writing home was done on a Friday afternoon. The Sisters read the letters first before it was posted and they read any replies of course. You always had to write what they wanted to hear. You never got the chance to say how unhappy you were. But things were getting better, we had more contact with the outside world and more freedom too that many of the girls from the past never had.

There was beginning to be a more relaxed atmosphere within the school when Canon Kelly came. We no longer had to form lines for meal times or bed time. Whenever a Sister drew our attention to them we could walk out the room and go to the refectory or the dormitory. For Mass, the first line of 6 year olds would go first then the line of the next age group up to the 16 year olds. Whenever we wanted to go to the toilet we had to ask permission in fact permission had to be sought for almost everything but things started to become less strict.

When I had turned twelve every Wednesday I joined three other girls in the workroom and darned socks for all the children of St John's from 4 - 6 p.m. Every week day a different group of four girls would darn. I remember us sitting on benches with our wooden mushrooms darning socks with wool and darned without talking or signing. We used to prick ourselves with those big needles and get scolded for not being quick enough. For working in silence for two whole hours we would have made very good Carmelite nuns!

Nothing much changed in the classroom until I had reached my fourteenth birthday. My mother complained about they way my hair was cut, of course it wasn't cut properly just a bunch of hair grabbed in one hand and cut off so it was all straggly and very short. Annie the lady who worked in the workroom and looked after our clothes was the one given the task to fine comb our hair and never cleaned the comb, she used the same one on every girl so as a result my hair was 'live' when I went home for the school holidays. My mother went along to the Education Department to complain and taking me along with her for the Director of Education to witness the state of my hair. I returned to school after missing an whole term as a result of my hair being 'live'. After that my hair was never fine combed by Annie or cut again.

The next term I returned to St John's Sister Barbara gave us a lecture on how to wash our hair. I am not surprised as Sister Martha who was in charged of bath time, and gave out our weekly clean clothes, never gave us a chance to wash our hair properly. As soon as we wet our hair she ordered us out of the bath. I had to dry my hair with a towel and it had not even been washed with shampoo. It also happened when she filled the bath with four inches deep of water and as soon as we sat in we were told to get out. Sister Martha would draw the curtain of the cubicle where the bath was and if we were naked in front of her she used to mutter something and make the sign of the cross. I often wondered if she had seen the devil and not me. She used to accuse me of being immodest so the next time I sat in the bath with my dressing gown! I couldn't understand what was wrong with my body or that I shouldn't look at it or spend time sponging my body with soap and water. When I grew older she never came in the bath cubicle again and that didn't bother me so I could spend time bathing myself properly and wash my hair properly too. Those ridiculous rules on modesty were to remain with me long after I left St John's. This behaviour from the Sisters gave most of us girls an inferiority complex.

When the Bishop of Leeds visited, I had only known him to visit once in my 8 years at St John's, all of us girls couldn't believe our eyes when we went into the refectory. The little girls jaws dropped. There were tablecloths laid on the tables, plates of ham sandwiches, cakes, Jellies and ice cream and even bread and jam were plentiful. We had glasses with lemonade too. That is the only time I have ever seen a display of such food at St John's. I remember the Bishop standing in the middle of the refectory saying grace in his magnificent robes and the Sisters queued up to kneel at his feet to kiss his holy ring. When the bishop was not visiting we had a slice of stale bread that was hardly buttered and a cup of tea. At breakfast we were always served porridge, there was always a lashing of syrup on the top. The Sisters gave it to their favourite ones. We had mainly stews for dinner, the dumplings and the lumps of grizzle were not very appetising but we had no choice but to eat it. Food was very scarce at St John's, we were always hungry and there were never any fat girls at St John's compared to today's obese. The Sisters used to give us a spoonful of cod liver oil daily to bring some colour to our pale faces.

 The little ones couldn't stomach the stews, the Sisters used to hold their noses, pinching so it hurt, until they just had to swallow because they had to breathe. It was a very upsetting sight to see.

Sometimes on a Saturday us older girls used to shell peas and peel potatoes, we often wondered what happened to the peas as we never saw them at meal times. Perhaps they were for the Sisters. So the next time we shelled peas we used to eat as many as we could. Sister Bernadette replaced Sister Catherine in the refectory and the way the little ones were treated at meal times didn't happen again as Sister Bernadette was a much nicer Sister.

As I grew older we were given other tasks to do. The older girls had to help the Sisters get the little ones up and put them to bed. They were in a large dormitory in the Sisters' quarters. I felt so sorry for the little ones, the three to four year olds were placed in cots and left to cry to sleep. After a while they got the message no one would come if they cried. Whatever love the Sisters were capable of feeling for their religion it certainly didn't extend to the children in their care. When I was fourteen a little boy of three came to the school. He was profoundly deaf. His name was Laurence Hayes. I used to get him up in the mornings and strip his cot of wet sheets so the Sisters would not smack him for wetting his bed. I put him to bed in the evenings with a cuddle as well. He was always looking out for me as his big sister. I am sure he missed his Mum and siblings at home greatly. He was one very confused little boy unaware of his fate. A year later all this was to change when they built a nursery unit next to the girls building and it was out of bounds so I did not see Laurence until the holidays. Laurence lived in Cheltenham so we were on the same train home for the holidays. We travelled from Leeds to Birmingham where a lot of children got off and then Lawrence and I were the only ones on the train heading for Bristol. There were no teachers to help us, we were just put on trains with labels on our coats so we would not get lost and the porter was supposed to look after us. I looked after Laurence on our journeys to and from school during holiday times and term times until I left school. I used to get him off the train at Cheltenham and hand him to his mother with his suitcase and jump back on the train for my journey to Bristol and on to Weymouth. She was always very grateful to me for looking after Laurence. When she visited him at school she always took me out for the day with Laurence. When I visited St John's in 1962 Laurence was eight years old and I went to see him in the classroom. "Do you remember me Laurence" I had said. He looked at me for a moment and said "the train". I wonder how he got on with his life on leaving school. I have tried to trace him over the years with no luck.

My maternal grandmother who lived in Lancashire, a staunch protestant, was not happy leaving me at St John's when she visited as she could see how unhappy I was. When I went to stay with her for a week at Easter I must have upset her greatly hiding in the coal shed outside and refused to open it. I refused to return to St John's and she used to say that if I did not go back the Sisters would not let me come again for the Easter holidays. She urged my parents to do something about it. After that I was offered a place at the Mary Hare Grammar School for the Deaf in Newbury, Berks. My Paternal Grandfather who was a Catholic did everything in his power to make me remain at St John's. The Mary Hare wasn't a Catholic School he said. I remember the tears streaming down my face when I begged to leave St John's and to be nearer home, he was proud of being a Catholic nothing would change his mind. As head of the family as Grandparents sometimes were looked upon in those days my parents went along with his wishes no matter how upset I was. It would have been a golden opportunity to go there as I would have had a better education and as it was in the South of England would have been much closer to home.

When I was thirteen I decided I had enough. We were incarcerated in that playroom and apart for some lessons during week days we stood around doing nothing at week-ends, went to chapel or cleaned. I used to dread the week-ends except the once a term visit to my Grandmothers. The playroom had no chairs except one little table and four chairs for the smallest children to sit on. There was ever only one large chair that was somehow raised and the Sister in charge sat on it looking over at us girls. No after school activities or books to read. There was no t.v. in those days except a wireless but only the Sisters could hear what was on. It was quite a large playroom and in the winter the only heat we had to keep warm was a small fire burning on one side. When the Sister in charge was busy putting coal on the fire in the playroom and had unlocked the door to the outside coal bunker for another girl to fill the coal bucket I sneaked out pretending to help. I went down the corridor where the coal was stored left the bucket there and got out through a door that led across to the laundry and I went out through one of other doors that one of the Sisters must have forgotten to lock. I found myself in one of the big fields. Freedom at last I thought, I knew my way as we used to help the Sisters lay sheets in the field to dry in summer time. I ran across the fields and climbed over the gate to get onto the main road. I walked past Bramham and tried to remember where the bus went when my grandmother came to take me home for the Easter holidays but then realised I had no money. It was getting dark and I was cold without a coat, I saw some lights in the distance, I walked up a muddy path which led to the farmhouse. I could see the farmers wife at the window and hesitated at first then went up and knocked on the door. She answered and led me into the kitchen. My shoes were all dirty from walking over the fields and my face was flushed from crying. I had fallen a few times as due to my hearing loss my balance in the dark is not very good. I gave her a piece of paper with my Grandmothers address and a phone number to contact her. My maternal Grandmother lived in Lancashire and visited on a Saturday afternoon once a term without fail where I had the luxury of sitting in the parlour with her and chatting. The Sisters used to bring her a cup of tea and a sandwich which she let me eat. Well, the farmer's wife must have known I came from the Deaf Institution from the way I talked and how I did not understand her. She put her arms around me saying not to worry and she went out of the kitchen with the piece of paper. I dried my tears and felt so much better knowing she had gone to contact my Grandmother and that I would soon be home safe with her. After a while the farmer's wife came into the kitchen where I was with her coat on and said everything would be alright and to come with her to the car. I went outside and sat in the car at the front next to her. After about 20 minutes I could see us driving up the entrance to St John's. My heart was pounding. I was struggling to get out of the car but she held me back. She persuaded me to come with her to the door, trying to reassure me everything was going to be alright then she rang the bell and Sister Barbara answered as if she was expecting us. We went in the parlour very nicely furnished and warm compared to our playroom which was bare, cold and depressing. Sister Barbara smiled at the farmers wife and put her arms across my shoulder in an apparently affectionate gesture and when she had gone grabbed me by the upper arm and marched me into Mother Superior's office. Mother Superior was Sister Clare at the time and she looked at me with her mouth firmly tucked in and a look of bitter discontent on her face. There I was told I was a disgrace to St John's. I was caned severely. You just couldn't run away again, you just wouldn't dare.

I told my parents about that incident explaining why I had run away and showed them the scars on my legs and hands. I was kept away for a term while it was investigated by the Education Department but the Sisters were always trying to absolve themselves from any blame. I returned to school the following term.

The back of St John's and the muddy fields that I ran over when I ran away from St John's. I arrived at the road in the foreground turned right that led me to a farmhouse some four miles away.

After I returned from a term away I came back to St John's to find we had a new Sister and her name was Sister Louise. She was one of the nicest sisters I had known and the youngest of them all. She taught a class of 7 to 9 year olds and helped with the general running of the school after school hours. She also introduced knitting for us. I made myself a blue jumper one winter, knitting every evening after school when I could and so did five other girls. It was great to knit after all we did was stand around in the playroom. One of the girls used to go to the cinema during the school holidays that she always came back to school with stories of the films she had seen and it made great entertainment as we assembled around her and she signed the stories to us.

One Sunday in the chapel at the age of fourteen I was feeling faint, Sister Barbara looked at me and realised I was so pale she took me out into the Sisters dining room, which was next to the chapel, for a glass of water. The day before I had polished the floor in three classrooms to a glass like shine with my bare hands as some of the girls had gone home for half term and as I lived so far away I had to stay. I had done my usual cleaning in the dormitory that Sunday morning and felt unwell. The other girl who was helping had run off to breakfast so I quickly finished it off for fear of getting told off. I was late for breakfast so had to go without. It was just suffocating not being able to go outside for some fresh air. Sister Barbara left me there for ten minutes and I looked around to see a long table with a white tablecloth, serviettes, silver knives and forks and side plates and water jugs and glasses. Also silver salt and pepper pots. There was a large jug of orange juice and grapefruit juice. I guess it was all ready laid out for their breakfast after Mass and that it had consisted of cereal, fruit juice and perhaps fried egg and bacon as there on the side table was a dome shaped silver dish with steam coming out and it smelt of fried bacon. I don't remember ever eating an egg at St John's or any fruit whatsoever. All we had for breakfast was watery porridge with a spoonful of syrup if you were lucky! I remember pieces of broken toast to share around and I wonder if they were leftovers from the Sisters breakfast. After witnessing what I saw in the Sisters dining room I felt a feeling of resentment at the Sisters overindulgence in contrast to their meanness towards us.

On one of my Grandmother's visits she brought a tape measure to measure me up for a bridesmaid dress. My Uncle, my grandmother's youngest son was getting married and he and his fiancée wanted me to be a bridesmaid. She had been measuring me when Sister Barbara came into the parlour and it was mentioned that there was going to be a wedding in the family. Sister Barbara said I could not be a bridesmaid as they were non catholics and I could not be a bridesmaid in a non catholic church. I can imagine the clashes that arose between Sister Barbara and my Grandmother. I was told firmly I could not be a bridesmaid. I was disappointed as since I had been at St John's I had missed so many family weddings and I had never been a bridesmaid. Nothing more was said until my Uncle's wedding day was approaching and I was allowed to attend the wedding but I was upset to be told I was not to be a bridesmaid. I went home to my Grandmother's for the wedding. There spread out on the bed at my Grandmother's was the most beautiful bridesmaid dress in pale blue. My Grandmother said I was going to be a bridesmaid and not to mention anything of it once I was back at St John's. The controlling attitude of the Sisters about religion with my mother's side of the family who were non catholics remained throughout my time at St John's. The Sister's racist attitude was unbelievable as Jesus himself on the Sermon on the Mount welcomed everyone of any race or creed.

A bridesmaid at my Uncle's wedding aged 14

Some of the girls who left at fifteen had neither a home to go to or any job. Some of them came back to St John's and were know as lodgers. That arrangement had been going on for years. They worked in the laundry under the watchful eye of Sister Gertrude and I believe that paid for their keep. Canon Kelly did not think that there should be a place for them in a school for deaf children so made arrangements for the young women to leave. In his view things were going to have to change and it was not an Institution any more but a School for the deaf.

In my later years at St John's we went on hiking trips with the lay teachers to the Peak District. We were able to see the beautiful vast countryside and to be out in the fresh air was wonderful and to be free from the Institution. We stayed in Youth hostels and we met up with hearing children who used to stare at us as if we came from outer space or maybe our sign language fascinated them.

For the first five years at St John's I don't

remember learning very much. I do wonder even today if those sisters were trained teachers of the deaf. There was no recreation in the playroom after school, no books to read or any kind of craft until Sister Louise came.

In summer, our class used to go down to the weir on the River Wharfe at Boston Spa with a lay teacher taking our easels with us to sketch. it was great to be out of the classroom and outside in the fresh air.

Canon Kelly arranged for a small library to be installed which was built in the corner of the hall with two steps leading up to a glass door into a small library measuring approximately 10 feet by 12. There was a desk and a typewriter in the library and it was there that I first learnt to type on those manual ones. The keys were made of steel and very hard to press then and if you made a mistake you had to be very careful when rubbing out so as not to make a hole in the paper! I helped Sister Barbara to keep the library tidy and to put books back on the shelves. It was great to see books and to be able to learn to read. So school life was not as hard or boring as when I first came to St John's. However time was running out for me. I had a little under a year before leaving school. Then Sister Barbara said as my birthday fell two weeks after the school term I could not leave in the summer of 1958 when I was 16 with all my friends. I thought I could have left at Christmas but I had to go back to St John's for another year.

I never had any speech therapy at St John's. When I went deaf at the age of eight my vocabulary was very limited so as I entered my adolescent years and adulthood I was unable to pronounce new words. When I went to St John's I could talk and when I left I could not talk properly. I used to think of the reasons why I was sent to a deaf school for specialist education and where my parents thought taught hearing and speech therapy and there didn't seem anything special about it. The appalling education when I first entered St John's was so obvious. Later on in my teens a classroom was converted into what they called a Hearing Room where there were headphones and audio equipment. I never went in one of those rooms, I had to stay behind and study the four gospels instead. I am sure they thought as I could not hear it was not worth me going into that room for hearing or speech therapy that they concentrated on those who had a little hearing. Only a few of the girls were hard of hearing or had little hearing and they were the ones that could listen to music in that room and be helped with their speech. In later years when I met my husband he helped me a great deal correcting the way I pronounced words, he helped me with controlling my voice either high or low and loud and quite. When I went back to visit St John's in the 60's Sister Barbara said I was talking so much better than when I was at school.

One of the best years at St John's was the year before I left school. Aged 16 I was able to go out into the village with another girl and get the ingredients for the Domestic Science Class. We took a list and bought the ingredients at the village grocer shop. We were one of the first girls to be allowed out on our own. The Sisters used to time us of course, we went straight there and back. That didn't matter the short time of freedom outside was better than nothing. Looking back that must have been the Sisters way of introducing us to the outside world so we would not be so institutionalised on leaving.

Cookery class St John's

When I came back after the Summer holidays in 1957 I found there were four boys in my class. There were six girls and four boys altogether in Sister

Barbara's Class. We were the first pupils of St John's to study for our G.C.E. exams and we were mostly taught by Sister Barbara. The boys were escorted over by Sister Margaret or Sister Kevin and Sister Barbara made sure they went back to the boys building after class. It was the first time in the schools history that boys and girls were integrated.

The classroom at St John's aged 14. Back row from left to right: Pauline Holmes, Wendy Higgins, Jean Vose, Peter Frain, Kathleen Forward (me). Front row from left to right: Con Mc Stay, Paddy Coleman, Michael Jenkinson, Catherine Stewart and Sister Barbara Walsh MBE

When I was 16 and in my last year at St John's one boy who was also 16 used to sneak out of the boys building to come and see me in my classroom around 8 p.m. where I studied in the evenings and that was out of bounds. I will never know how he knew me or how he knew where I would be studying in the evenings as we had no contact with the boys except a glimpse of them in the chapel. We used to talk about the studying I was doing and leaving St John's and how we couldn't wait to do so. I always held my breath when he came unexpectedly as if any Sister caught us we would be punished. I always used to tell him to please go. He had been working in the kitchens scrubbing pots and pans and sneaked out while the sisters were in chapel. I had quite often seen boys through the scullery hatch when I was clearing tables in the refectory after supper. You could never have a chance to talk to the boys with the Sisters always watching us. After a while he never came again. I guess he was caught and I can imagine the punishment he must have had. Boarding schools in the 50's were a lot harsher than they are today.

In my last year at St John's I studied the Four Gospels which were Matthew, Mark, Luke and John and no other subjects. Canon Kelly had made so many changes in the schools curriculum and there was not enough time for me to study for my G.C.E. in English, Maths, and History before I left school. I had to spend all my time on the gospels during school hours, in the evenings after supper and before bedtime too. There was little time for anything else. I passed my 'O' Levels in Scripture. Where on earth can you get a job with Scripture unless you want to be a nun of course. Did they think I was going to be a nun? Well I did live the life of a novice during the last two years at St John's. Mass three times a week and Mass & Benediction on Sundays and prayers morning and night. I was one of the first girls to take G.C.E. exams and it was a credit to St John's and the Sisters that I passed. Pity it had not come to St John's earlier as I had only time to study one subject. I did take practical cookery and needlework 'O' level before I left as well.

    The last Christmas I was to spend at St John's we had a Christmas party one evening for the 15 - 16 year olds. The hall was decorated and there was a Christmas Tree in the corner. Sister Margaret allowed the boys to smarten up because I noticed they were really smart when they came over to the girls school hall which was just off the parlour. The girls were able to put their glad rags on. It was terribly daunting when the girls entered the hall as all the boys were huddled together in one corner, so us girls were and huddled together in the other. We had no idea what we were supposed to do. It was so awkward as we had been told never to look at boys and this was our first time in the presence of a boy at St John's. Sister Margaret and Sister Kevin were there from the boys side and Sister Barbara and Sister Louise from the girls. After feeling a bit relaxed the boys spread out but remained on one side. Sister Margaret made sure we didn't cross over but we were able to sign messages over to each side. There were little sandwiches and cakes and soft drinks. Canon Kelly came in and tried to get us to mingle but the Sisters were having non of that. He however managed to get a few of us to have a waltz with both partners keeping a visible distance. He gave a demonstration of how to waltz with Sister Kevin as his partner. It didn't last long and it was sad as we were just beginning to enjoy the evening even though the Sisters were watching us. When the hour was up we were given a little Christmas present each and Sister Margaret went over to the boys, one by one pulling them by the arm, and marched them all out which was totally unnecessary. She could have spared them the embarrassment by just asking them to leave. The girls stayed to clear up and I could see the boys being escorted down the corridor past the chapel by Sister Margaret shoving them along into the boys building.

I remember we spent more time praying and cleaning at St John's than actually getting an education. The wooden floors throughout the institution shone like glass! No one ever came in from outside to do all the domestic chores, the girls had to do them. For my time at St John's I worked in the refectory washing up with three other girls for about 2 years, then I did the dormitories which floors were mopped every morning before class for 2 years. Every Saturday we had to give all the dormitories a good clean. We collected tea leaves from the kitchens and spread it out in a row on the floor then swept it moving the row across the floor. There was never any social activities or any plans for the week-ends, all we did was clean and pray. Younger girls were polishing the staircase too. After two years on the dormitories I cleaned the wooden floors in the classrooms for the last two years at St John's. Every girl was given different duties of cleaning to do. I remember the tins of wax and how I had to scrape it off with a cloth and spread it on the floors on a Saturday, that had to be put on first then we had those heavy iron blocks with a polishing cloth underneath that were as heavy as weights and attached to blocks was a long stick and we had to push them back and forth until the floor shined. I am sure the Sisters found lots of cleaning for us as they must have thought the devil found work for idle hands.

Even in the coldest winters we played hockey in the fields or netball in the playground. The girls from the other convents in the area used to come and play against us. When they went off the pitch to go back to their respective schools we went inside and we used to think of the freedom they had going home after school. It wasn't long before we were able to go to other schools. It was exciting to be out, free from the Institution and being given some sense of normality in our school lives.

In the chapel on Sundays and on other days of obligation the boys were at one side at the back and the girls were at another side in the front. The sisters sat in the back rows watching over us. We were never allowed to look at the boys, if we did we had to write that in our confessions. The boys usually left the chapel before us but on the occasions we left first we had to join our hands together, eyes cast downwards to the floor and walk out of the chapel. You wouldn't dare lift your head up. I used to think this sort of behaviour was very strange and it had made me have an inferiority complex as when I left St John's I was afraid to look at men and boys.

    We used to go to confession on a Saturday so we had clean souls for holy communion on the Sunday. I don't know what we could confess when we couldn't do anything wrong with the sisters closely watching over us. I could never think of what to write. We used to write our confessions on a piece of paper and hand it to the priest in the confession box. Some of the girls could not read or write so they copied the ones that could. I am sure the priest must have thought they were all the same. The only difference was if one had put that I looked at the boys 6 times they would write 8 times or another number. The priest never said that was not a sin. After that he used to give us one Our father and five Hail Mary's as penance.

The ridiculous religious teaching must have brainwashed us all as when studying the bible most of what they taught was not even written. Indeed my last two years at St John's I lived the life of a novice. Twenty five of us girls slept in cubicles which consisted of three walls and one wall was curtained off. There in the cubicles was a bed, a locker and rug (the rugs were made by us older girls). A Crucifix or holy picture was on the wall above our bed. It was like sleeping in a box. Canon Kelly and Sister Barbara had arranged for them all to be pulled down the Summer I left school so when the girls returned to St John's there was a more open space and homely feel about the dormitories where they could have all their own possessions like clothes and pictures and even a duvet of their own choice. It was no longer like a convent but a proper boarding school.

The weeks turned into days and soon I was going to leave. I was getting excited as my time at St John's was like a prison sentence. I was totally unprepared for the outside world. We had no sex education, it was never talked about by the Sisters and when we asked questions the subject was changed. I was 16 when my grandmother told me husband and wives shared beds. I remember thinking how wonderful, the warmth and the company but what else they might do stayed a mystery. I searched the bible, it wasn't much help. I asked Sister Barbara and she said **God made me** so I never asked another question again.

I left St John's in July 1959 two months before my 17th birthday. The Sisters saw us off at Leeds train station. The evening prior to my leaving the Sisters were giving a talk to the school leavers saying to take great care, there was a wicked world out there they said. We were not to socialise with non catholics or even marry a non catholic man. I remember feeling afraid as we were going out into the unknown. We were given a rosary and a statue of Mary. That night I could barely sleep and my mind travelled back to the day when I first entered St John's as a very frightened eight year old, now I was going to leave and I had no idea what life lay ahead of me. I was still awake at daybreak and then watched the sun rise. When the Sister came in to pull our bedcovers back, as she had been doing for eight long years since I came into St John's, I was thinking it would be the last day. I knelt by my bed to say my morning prayers and I continued to do that long after I left school as it had become a habit. I quickly dressed in my own clothes and a pair of shoes that my Grandmother had bought me a few weeks previously to wear when leaving school. With them I wore my first pair of stockings a teacher had given me for keeping her classroom clean for two years. I was so glad to leave those black ankle socks and black shoes behind. I was going to miss my Grandmother but I vowed I would come back to visit her one day when I had saved enough from my first job. I had breakfast in the refectory, the usual porridge, tea and toast for the last time and thought how much it had changed since the day I first came. After having breakfast I went upstairs to the dormitory and the classroom to pick up my meagre possessions I had whilst at St John's and went into the hall downstairs to find my suitcase where the Sisters had organised in groups. One for Manchester, Newcastle, Birmingham and London. I was with the Birmingham group and once many of the children got off at Birmingham Laurence and I were the only ones left in the train carriage. After Laurence was met by his mother at Cheltenham I was the only one travelling far South as I had been in my entire eight years at St John's. Many of them lived in nearby towns to each other and kept in touch, I couldn't do that as I lived too far away.

 I travelled the long train journey home alone and looking after Laurence for the last time. I wonder how he managed his journeys after that, I am sure his mother was very anxious. I was old enough the Sisters said to take the train from Bristol to Weymouth and catch the boat home. It was a night boat I remember and I slept on a bench for 6 hours. I had a packed lunch and some orange juice the

Sisters had given me the morning of my departure and twice as much as the other children as I had a longer journey. I saved some for when I was on the boat. The Sisters had given me my train and boat ticket and directions and that was all I needed. I walked a long way from the station to Weymouth harbour, with my suitcase, remembering my way from the many journeys I had made with my father and in later years on my own. The train journey usually took all day and the boat journey all night in those days. I remember feeling the world outside seemed a very frightening place to be on ones own and at St John's it was a very safe place to be locked up by the Sisters. Years later I thought of the dangers I could have been in when you think of all the murders, abductions and rapes on young children and women in this world today.

Standing on deck I watched the boat move away from the harbour and I felt sad thinking of my school friends as we had lived like sisters and slept in the same dormitories. I thought of those friends who

I may never see again and that I had no idea what lay in store for me at home in Jersey. I watched the boat sail away until England was no more than a blur on the horizon. I sat on a bench on the boat and ate the sandwiches I had saved and looked up at the stars in the dark sky. The clouds of smoke were billowing out of the ships funnel as the boat headed across the channel. It was 11 p.m. and I would be home at 6 a.m. the next morning. Passengers were hurrying along the deck and going downstairs to their cabins. I stayed where I was on a bench on the deck for fear of losing my seat. It was July and there was just a chill in the night air from the sea. I put my coat on and wrapped it around me, soon I lay down on a bench to sleep. When I woke up it was daybreak and the sea was calm. Passengers were coming up from the cabins having spent the night sleeping in a bunk. Seagulls were flying around the boat as if to navigate it. I could see land in the distance and knew I would soon be home.

The front of St John's today.

St John's
Catholic School for the Deaf
Boston Spa, Yorkshire

Modern logo for the school today.

Life After St John's

When the boat moored in the harbour I looked out for my family. I couldn't see them so I thought they would be a little late. Passengers were disembarking off the boat and I picked up my suitcase and followed. I waited on the harbour for my Mother as I was told in a letter a month ago at school that my Father was in hospital. My Mother didn't come so I picked up my suitcase and started to walk home. We lived about two miles away from the harbour. On arriving home I found my father was in bed resting. He had just come home from hospital the day before. He told me Mother had left and was not coming back and that he was divorcing her. I was upset as I had missed her, it was a time when I needed my mother most and I had been looking forward to leaving school and going home to be with my family. My eldest brother had joined the army. My little brother who was ten at the time was at school and the brothers of De La Salle College were taking good care of him. I was so pleased to see him looking well when he came home from school.

Sister Barbara was my housemother and my teacher from the day I entered St John's to the day I left. When I left St John's in 1959 quite unprepared for the outside world I came home to nothing. After the way we were brought up at St John's I had a terrible inferiority complex that did nothing for my self esteem when I entered the hearing world on leaving school. There were no social workers in those days to help me. I wrote to Sister Barbara to tell her how things were and she wrote back and said to come back and they would give me a job there until things got better. I just couldn't go back no matter how bad things were. I couldn't leave my father who was a very poorly man and my ten year old brother too.

I was starting my young life with plenty of sorrow. I tried to put St John's and the Sisters out of my mind. I had been institutionalised and was finding it very hard to adjust in the hearing world. My father drank heavily to block out his problems, his health and his divorce. He was frequently going in and out of hospital. I looked after my father and my little brother and tried to look for a job to no avail. One afternoon I went to see my Aunt Phyllis who was married to my fathers brother and broke down. Life had been hard at St John's but this was worse. My Aunt was a very outspoken woman and would not take any nonsense. In fact my Aunt Phyllis and Uncle Bernard were very good people, always willing to help the family. I had been home since July and it was now December and I had no job, no income or any hope for the future. I didn't have a social life either, spending time at home looking after my father and my young brother. My Aunt took me the next day to the Education Department as she felt the authorities were responsible for sending me away to a special school now they could do something to help, she said. My Aunt had already tried to help coming along to interviews for jobs but we were not very successful. She had already bought me clothes for that purpose.

At the Education Department, after a long talk with the Director of Education, my Aunt and myself it was decided I go back to school, attending the 6th form at St Helier Girls in the afternoons to study English, English Literature and typewriting and later when Highlands College opened I moved there. I did not want to go back to school but I had no choice. After St John's it was very daunting going to a hearing school where there were large classes of 30 pupils compared to St John's classes were small and had 10 to 12 pupils. The Director of Education told my Aunt they would give me a job in the mornings at the Education Department doing clerical work. Things were getting too much at home with my fathers drinking and looking after my little brother that my Aunt offered to have my brother and myself for meals during the week. I went to see the headmistress the week before attending the school and was given a school uniform. Not a new one but my father did not have much money so that had to do. At least it was much better than the one at St John's.

Sitting here today looking back over the years that have passed all too quickly it is incredible that I was sent away to a special school and here I was at the age of seventeen going back to school. St John's wasn't a school, it was an Institution when I first went there. It took five years before many of the changes were made gradually that I only had two years of proper schooling and a lot to catch up on. Many deaf children today are not sent to special schools on the mainland but go to mainstream school where there are special classes. It came all too late for me. When I was attending St Helier Girls some of the girls in my class were the friends I had made in primary school. It seemed as if I was waking up from a bad dream after eight years. Did the education authorities in those days ever visit St John's or even read the school reports realising it was not a school but an Institution?

I did a year at St Helier Girls School and did well passing all my exams. I am not going to say it was easy. The teachers used to talk to the class for an hour and then when everyone was doing their writing she used to come over and help me one to one or sometimes the other pupils sitting next to me used to let me copy their notes. The teachers used to help me with speech too and indeed they were not special teachers of the deaf or even speech therapists. After a year I left St Helier Girls and the Education Department where I was working part time offered me a full time job. I also went to Highlands College in the evenings to pick up on my reading and typewriting.

As well as attending Church regularly after I left school I went to confession every week after leaving St John's. The Sisters made it clear to me that if I did not go to church or confession I would be committing a mortal sin. After a while the priest must have been fed up reading the same strange confessions written on a piece of paper every week.

He must have thought I had some form of mental retardation. I could not think what to write remembering the priest at St John's had never told us what was a sin and what was not. "There was no need to come to confession anymore" the young priest said on my usual visit to the confessional one Saturday. I was deaf he said so he would give me total absolution for the rest of my life so after that I never went again.

Marriage

I met my husband James in January 1960 a year after I left school. We met outside the church where we had been for a church service. We started dating and spent many happy times together whenever we could. He was my best friend and helped me enormously in my life after St John's. We married two years later in June 1962 and I continued to work at the Education Department.

In July 1965, three years after our marriage, we had a son and another son followed in June 1968. After the birth of my second son James priority in life was drink. He went out most evenings and became irresponsible. He never wanted to go out with us as a family. I was spending too long at home alone with my sons and the only time I went out was when I took them to the park or shopping. He started seeing other women that our marriage went downhill despite the positive start. He became abusive towards me, treated me with such mental cruelty. I thought after life at St John's need I want more so I divorced him. He remarried of course and left Jersey so with my sons we moved on with our lives.

It was indeed very hard to go out to work and bring up two boys on my own but if any parent succeeded in doing this, deaf or not then so could I. It was a lonely life but I was busy working and had my sons to bring up and care for. I know they missed having their father around and I had to be a mother and father to them. The years soon passed and they grew up very quickly and life became a lot easier. They were doing well at school and had won a scholarship to a Public school here in Jersey.

The eldest went on to University to study medicine and my youngest went on to College to study accountancy. I am very proud of them to this day. The eldest is now a Consultant in a U.K. hospital. My youngest is now working for a bank in Spain. Both sons are doing very well in their present lives, both are married and I am the proud Grandmother of five little boys. I don't see them as much as I would like to, they have very busy lives that I have to keep in touch with them in case I am forgotten.

My Working Life

After my divorce and my sons were at school I went back to work. I worked for a firm of accountants as an accounts typist for 12 years. There I was happy and loved my job though there were difficulties with communication. When an accountant wanted something typing such as a spreadsheet they were too afraid or shy to come and ask me so went to the next person in the typing pool and then it was summed up in one simple sentence what they had wanted done. How was I to know the details. A lack of communication was the problem as if something went wrong then of course it was 'the deaf lady's' fault! I had been in the job twelve years when they decided to get a supervisor to add to the four of us in the typing pool. It was then things started to go wrong. I was told I was holding things up and the work wasn't flowing quick enough, again of course it was all my fault so they asked me to take a less responsible job within the firm or leave. Of course it had to to be me and not a hearing person and it was then I realised the discrimination and bullying coming to the surface. One was married and taking so much time off with her children being sick or whatever but of course it had to be me, a deaf person holding things up. The supervisor herself used to walk in at 10 o'clock in the mornings when if I was five minutes late I am told 'can you come in at nine'! Not forgetting to take into account the lunch hours I had worked or the times I left the office late in the afternoons. Accountants used to come up to me and talk to me behind my back knowing I was deaf. I had worked with many of them for twelve years so did they know a deaf person can only understand what they are saying if they are talking to my face. When asked to repeat they just went away, so many people are impatient if you don't understand them straight away. It is always concluded that it is difficult for the hearing person, what makes them think it is any easier for a deaf person? They could have put pen to paper and left a note attached. Lip reading can be very tiring. They had always been like that for the entire twelve years I had worked there so it was confusing as to why it was brought up after all this time. I was really struggling to bring up and support my family on my own income so I accepted their offer of alternative employment within the firm, not wanting to be unemployed. I couldn't believe what they had given me, a filing job in the basement working on my own in a cold downstairs room! I didn't feel they had any respect for me as a deaf person. If you can hear you could get a small portable radio and listen and keep busy but for me it was silent. I stayed one week and left as it was so depressing. Of course they gave me a good reference stating I was an excellent typist and worked hard, no mention was made as to why they moved me from the job I had actually applied for twelve years previously. In the workplace when someone like a supervisor or personal officer came to talk to the department or a group I was working with I cannot hear and they well knew that and when I questioned what the talk was about they summed it up in one simple sentence. This lack of communication made it all the more difficult to fit in with the work.

Then I applied for a job at a firm of Lawyers. Going for an interview was daunting as there were no social workers in those days to help. I was offered a job nevertheless and I worked hard but then I suffered bullying and discrimination there too. I worked until 7 pm some evenings in the summer when they had wanted a court document for the next day typed out with numerous copies of the case printed off and I was always the one to volunteer to stay behind. No one else would offer. Luckily my sons were either at friends or at some after school activities. I wasn't even paid for the work! The staff never seemed to get anything finished on time but again the finger was always pointed at me because I was deaf and I was holding them up, so again after 3 years I was the one that had to go. I learnt a couple of months later that those working in the same office as me lost their jobs.

Supervisors often put me down and were very patronising. I found women Supervisors very ruthless. Being deaf has never been a problem for me, it's the way people chose to relate to me as a deaf person which has. How could they possibly understand what being deaf meant when they are not deaf themselves. There is so much stigma attached to deafness in this not so perfect world. It was ironic that the firm had been awarded a certificate of achievement for helping disabled people to work there or help find them employment when I was asked to go.

It was very difficult, in those days, being deaf in a hearing world, especially in the workplace. There was no deaf awareness training as there is today. Most supervisors were patronising. How could they possibly understand or know what it is like to be deaf when they are not deaf. I suffered from depression and it was a struggle to stay strong. I then decided to leave working in the private sector and enter the civil service. I knew I could do as well as the next person given the chance so I didn't give up looking for employment. Today there are more deaf people in the island than when I returned home from St John's. There is a social worker to help with any problems in the workplace today, which didn't happen in my working life.

After leaving the firm of lawyers I was unemployed for a year. I then went on to work in the civil service for the States of Jersey where I worked for 32 years. I was moving around on contract to several different States departments wherever there was work. I usually spent three years or more in any one department, moving to another for three years then going back again for a further three in some departments. My working life in the civil service did not go without problems. After the bullying and discrimination I suffered at the firm of Accountants and the firm of lawyers States departments were no exception. The bullying and discrimination I encountered would not happen today as anti bullying laws/discrimination law in the workplace are now in place. Neither would unfair dismissal too. I couldn't write about it all here as it would need another book! It does still exist as despite so much deaf awareness these days there are a certain minority who stick to their own belief that they know what deaf means.

My sons had left for University and College and eventually flew the nest. I continued working. I was experiencing the empty nest syndrome and life alone became lonely once my sons had left Jersey and got married. When I retired I took voluntary jobs at Durrell and the National Trust to get me out of the house. I love my voluntary job at Durrell where I am not treated any different and I have made many friends. However attending coffee mornings and talks create problems as I can't join in the conversations going on or the talks given by professionals so don't attend. Being deaf is indeed a lonely life when you are excluded from so many things in the hearing world. Deafness is something that most people misunderstand. If you were blind someone would go out of their way to help as you can obviously see that person is blind but deafness is a hidden disability. They look at you and think you are a normal person but once you explain you are deaf many just move away and talk to the next person leaving you isolated and alone. Body language and facial expressions can speak volumes. I would rather not attend social functions as there is nothing worse to dampen your self esteem to be left there standing like an idiot. When everyone laughs about something that is funny you don't know what is funny so you aren't laughing. By the time someone may explain it the novelty has worn off. I do wonder in my retirement how I got through those years in the workplace.

    I was invited to an evenings entertainment at a hotel with a colleague, she had persuaded me to come, you can watch the dancing, she said. When we arrived and took up our seats at the back there the entertainer was telling jokes. I didn't think I would be noticed amongst the crowd of 200 people in the room but after a while I was and how very embarrassing. He said to the audience 'that woman over there in a blue dress has not laughed at me all evening' my friend told me and she shouted out that I was deaf. He changed the subject quickly and went on to something else. Perhaps that will teach him to think before he speaks! It was so embarrassing that I never went to an evening like that again. I do try to mingle but once you tell people you are deaf and they can't understand what I say they move away. If they took the time and patience to listen and bring me in to conversations all would be well. Suffice to say life is busy for all of us and that includes me. Most people associate deafness with being stupid. My doctor told me that I talk very well for someone who is as deaf as I am. Thankfully there are still a few nice people who take the trouble and time to listen. It is very difficult to sit in an audience and try to lip read the person on stage, they are constantly moving their head and I can only understand and lip read people in one to one conversations.

I don't remember ever being bullied or discriminated at the Education Department in the years 1960 - 1965 when I first started work. It was when I returned to work in the 70's after my divorce and my sons were 6 and 3 years old and had started school that bullying and discrimination were rife in the workplace. Disabled people in whatever form are supposed to be brave and can put up with anything! We are easy victims to those bullies because of our disability. Unfortunately the unfair dismissal and anti-discriminations law was not in place when I was in the workplace. I learnt after leaving St John's that life as a deaf person in a hearing world is indeed hard and you have many obstacles to overcome.

In my final working years when I was three years to retirement I was working at the Psychology Department. The secretary decided to leave with her partner and emigrate to Australia. It was a very sad day for me when she left as we had worked very well together for seven years. A new lady much older than her had been interviewed and took her place. She had not been there very long when she went on holiday and a temporary member of staff was recruited from an agency to cover for her. One afternoon I told her that I would not be back after lunch until 3 p.m. as I had an appointment at the hospital at 2 p.m. Members of staff were entitled to an hour for doctors or hospital appointments even for the dentist so all I had to do is leave a message to say where I was. When I returned I was shocked to be confronted by the head of the department that I had been shopping! I said I had not been shopping but that I had an hospital appointment, showing her my appointments card I asked where she had got that from even though I already knew. Actually the temp was snowed under with work as she was new to the job and had been there a week, her job had nothing to do with me as I was only a part-time data inputter of patients records and checked files and put them away for the psychologists after their appointments. Well, she had told her that I had gone off shopping and she was snowed under with work. I explained what happened but things seemed to go in her favour and I was told by the head of department that she felt I was not in the right job and asked me to leave. I couldn't believe it when I had worked there for seven years. I did fight my case but at the time it was in June and anti-discrimination laws and unfair dismissal did not come into force until the following September so there was nothing I or anyone could do but hold my head high and leave. I was upset, I felt they did not want me there as being deaf it was a lot of work for them. To be honest if they took the time and trouble to speak to me properly and explain things I could work as the well as the next person but why after seven years!. If they had wanted me to help the temporary assistant I would have done so but her job wasn't in my job description. As I had three more years of my working life left I had hoped to stay there until retirement. I couldn't find another job due to my age and at the time there were many job losses in the island and people were unable to find work. The job centre could not help so I gave up finding another job. It messed up my pension and my life. Being deaf as well as my age at the time it was indeed hard to find other employment. Of course it had to be me to leave and not the temporary assistant who had been there a week. How could someone as intelligent as a Psychologist believe her story. Furthermore I was suffering from depression at the time and the very people that are supposed to help you were the very people that cost me my job. After that I never worked again.

I once attended a funeral of a colleague. The funeral director was handing out a hymn book to those entering the church for the funeral. I accepted one and put it down on the seat. Later when the hymns began I just stood there and the funeral director must have noticed I did not have a hymn book and that I wasn't singing so came over to give me one. Again I put it down on the seat. He was waving his arms conducting the hymns sung looking in my direction and again came over to give me another hymn book. I felt so embarrassed and walked out of the service. If only people could think for a minute. Deafness is a hidden disability. I didn't get the chance to speak to him in his ear to tell him I was deaf but then he wouldn't have understood anyway.

I will be honest to admit I don't go to church much now, I just can't follow the service. The congregation join in where they say one sentence and the priest says another. I just sit or stand there looking dim! In any case I have had enough of church when I was at St John's to last me a lifetime! People I have spoken to about how difficult it is to follow at Mass say - well, you can read the prayer book! How inconsiderate of them. A deaf person has to sit through a church service not knowing what is said or going on while others are joining in the service and I am left out of the service! I know many deaf people who have left St John's and given up their faith. I am still a believer in prayer, I am still a christian, it is just that I can see no harm saying your own prayers at home without going into a church.

They do put in loop systems for the deaf in churches nowadays but what good is it to me. I am sure it helps a hard of hearing person but not one who is severely deaf like me. The service was so much better in the olden days when you could follow, indeed it was at St John's but things have changed.

Brandy

On a visit to my son one afternoon we were talking about a new job he had been offered and moving to Spain to live and work there. At our feet was a little moggy called Brandy. He was tabby with a white chest and four years old and he sensed something was about to happen that he followed my son everywhere. He was absolutely adorable and he knew me from my visits to my son. We discussed what was going to happen to Brandy. He said he had friends who might take him or the shelter would find a home for him. I just couldn't bear the thought of never seeing him again. I was living in a top floor flat and decided to move into my sons house and look after Brandy whom I eventually adopted when my son had settled in Spain.

The day my son left he sent me a text to say Goodbye and that he had left the keys under the doormat. "Be good to Brandy he said, he is very nervous". Brandy was a rescue cat and did not have a good start in life, as a kitten he and his brother lived with an elderly gentleman who used a stick on them. They eventually went to the Animals Shelter in Jersey, Channel Islands where we live. My son wanting a cat went along to find one and picked him out. He was told he could not take just the one, Brandy had a brother, a ginger coloured one with exactly the same markings as brandy, where the tabby colouring was he was ginger. They had been together since birth and the shelter were not prepared to split them up. For that reason my son had to take both home. The ginger cat was three years old when he was hit on the main road by a passing car. I know my son was very fond of that cat. When he died Brandy used to sit outside the cat flap calling for his brother and no amount of persuading would make him come in. He needed to have a lot of fuss made of him to help him get over his loss when in fact they were inseparable.

The morning I arrived with my suitcase at my

sons house I found Brandy sitting on the sofa, he was staring ahead. I felt I knew how he was feeling as I was sad my son had left Jersey but he had lost his master with whom he had spent four happy years. He was very nervous but made no attempt to move from where he was sitting. I went over and stroked him and he looked at me with sad eyes not even jumping off the sofa as he would when visitors visited. I made a fuss of him and fed him but he was not interested in eating.

He refused to use his basket which was after four years new and the fluffy blanket I bought for him had never been slept on or washed. He slept anywhere he fancied. The house was his, he owned everything that in some ways I became his slave.

Brandy & I settled in together very well. He was my constant companion and indeed for the next five years. As I am profoundly deaf Brandy was very clever at understanding that I was not like my son who immediately let him out of the front door when he meowed, he had to come and tell me. By doing this he scratched my knee with his paw as he did when the doorbell rang. At night he used to come in the cat flap with his muddy paws, climb the stairs and insist he sleeps on my bed. He even shared the pillow with me. The sheets had to be washed almost everyday due to his muddy paw marks but that did not deter me from sharing my bed with him. In the mornings he used to wake me up with his paws stroking my cheeks. More often than not he would leave a present outside my bedroom door, the list was endless. A beautiful robin, a bird, a mouse, a shrew or even a hedgehog! You never knew what you would find the next morning. Sometimes I was up until 3 a.m. trying to catch a mouse that he had brought into my bedroom. He never really killed the mice but brought them in the house between his teeth through the cat flap, climbed the stairs then dropped them on the bedroom floor. I just couldn't tell him off as he used to look at you with such adorable innocent eyes as if to say 'why are you throwing out my presents'.

The neighbours next door had a new cat. Much to my delight he was very similar to Brandy's brother, ginger. He was a couple of years younger than Brandy but the two boys became best friends. They used to go into each others houses for sleepovers but the worst was Brandy used to eat his food but there was never any left in Brandy's bowl for his new friend to eat. As a result Brandy put on a lot of weight and his new friend was very slim. I had to put him on a diet. He had to squeeze through the cat flap and eventually stopped using it and sat and waited outside the door to be let in or if he was inside he used to scratch my knee as if to say 'I want to go out'.

When he wanted to remind me that it was dinner time he would go and sit by his empty bowl as if saying 'my bowl is empty' ….. or 'its dinner time' ….. or maybe 'I am hungry where is my food'. After dinner he would sit on my lap and have a nap until he wandered off through the cat flap. As the months went by he put on a lot of weight from having sneaked next door and eaten his friend's food. I had to cut his food by half and stop giving him treats. He was not very happy. One night he got in the kitchen cupboard, one of his clever tricks. He knocked down a jar of catnip and ate half the jar. His reward was that he was very sick the next morning and had slept all day. So every night I had to make sure the cupboards were shut tight.

One evening I decided to have a bath and go to bed and read. Brandy was outside and he usually came in at midnight or after so I thought I would have an early night. I closed the bedroom door and as I was reading facing the door I thought I had seen the door handle move. I watched it for a few seconds and it moved again. I was beginning to get frightened when all of a sudden the door opened with Brandy clinging to the door handle and swinging on it. His body was so long almost touching the floor. The door was usually open a little for him but on this occasion it was closed and he decided to open it himself. He then jumped on my bed and sat right in front of the book demanding attention.

Brandy hated his trips to the veterinary hospital and to have his teeth cleaned, scaled and polished. He was well looked after and healthy not forgetting how expensive vets fees were. He hated going in a box to the vets and travelling in the car. I had to lock the cat flap and catch him but he hid anywhere, in the wardrobe, under the bed, in the shower, I had to prepare at least an hour beforehand. I used to sit at the back with him and according to my friend who was driving he cried and cried. I would have loved to hear his little voice. When we collected him later that day after he had a dentist appointment his teeth were sparkling but he was not amused. Although he hated going in the box he was very quick getting back inside it as if he was jet propelled after the vet had examined him and given him his injections.

One morning I left the taps on in the kitchen and I was in the lounge. Brandy was coming back and forth from kitchen to lounge and then suddenly I noticed his paws were leaving wet prints on the wooden floor and I immediately guessed a tap was running and overflowing. He was very clever trying to tell me even though I was late in spotting it.

When I went on holiday he was left behind but he had his friend next door and a neighbour came in twice a day to feed him. He would have hated it in a cage at the cattery. When we got back he usually was upstairs on my bed and according to my friend who picked me up and drove me home he gave out the loudest meow as if to say 'where have you been'! He ran down the stairs to greet me and was always pleased to see me back.

One summer afternoon in July Brandy was outside and I had cleaned the kitchen floor. He was at the window and wanted to come in but I had wanted the floor to dry first. It was his evening meal time. I thought five more minutes would not do any harm. He wandered off fed up of waiting. The floor was dry and I put out his dinner in his little bowl with a bowl of water too. Half an hour later he had not come in so I went out to look for him. There on my driveway was poor Brandy sitting and staring into space, his face covered in blood. My first instinct was that he had a nosebleed. I picked him up and a friend rushed us to the veterinary hospital. The journey in the car seemed to take forever especially as it was rush hour. I was nursing him in his favourite blanket on my lap. I could feel his heart pounding. At the veterinary hospital, I walked in with Brandy and a vet nurse looked up from the reception desk, looking shocked at the sight of Brandy covered in blood pressed the emergency button for the vet to come out. The nurse immediately took him off me and went into the treatment room. I had to wait in the waiting room while they did some tests and an X-ray. The vet appeared and spoke to me very carefully as to not build up my hopes all was well. It was found that Brandy had been hit by a car as the x-ray showed tyre marks down the front of his face. He had a fractured scull and a haemorrhage. They kept him in overnight and the next day. After two days of trying to do everything to save my beloved pet, very early one morning the phone rang and a friend who was staying in the house at the time answered it as I could not. It was the vet who said they had done all they could to save him. Brandy had tried to get up to use his tray and had collapsed and died at 7 a.m. that morning. Despite his injuries he kept himself clean to the end.

It was like losing a child when he died and the weeks that followed were very hard now that I did not have Brandy to nurture and care for, or even have a purpose for getting up early to fill his bowl and let him out. I was devastated at losing my beloved pet. I used to see his little face everywhere, at the window, at the cat flap and even looking down at the kitchen floor I could see him there where he ate his food from his bowl. The morning he died I went to see him at the veterinary hospital. I was able to hold him and say goodbye. His body was very stiff and it broke my heart to hold him like that when he used to come right up to my chin and rub his against mine. The nurse said he was a very good cat, he was healthy and had beautiful fur that it was a shame he had passed away from his injuries. I arranged to have him cremated together with his favourite toy whale. He is now in a little box displayed at home. I will never forget him ever. I am glad that we had five happy years together, he was spoilt and I loved him. Had he not died from his injuries he could have lived another nine years as the vet said Brandy was a very healthy cat and was well looked after. He said I should remember that Brandy had a happy life with me.

The Vet at the Veterinary Hospital at Georgetown in Jersey gave me some leaflets and a contact address to get in touch with the Blue Cross Pet Bereavement Service in the United Kingdom. I did contact them and was put in touch with a counsellor. We corresponded on my laptop for four weeks and I don't know how I would have got through those four weeks had it not been for her. When Christmas came I sent them a card and a donation for their Charity in memory of Brandy.

Brandy gave me so much happiness and being

deaf he was my ears at home. He used to sit on a ledge on the high wall in the garden under the leaves of the ivy to have his afternoon nap on a hot summers day. A few days after he died the leaves rustled and moved in that very spot as if he was there. I just did not want to believe he had gone. He must now be over the rainbow somewhere.

The driver who had apparently been doing deliveries on the close where we live reversed on my drive and hit Brandy. Brandy must have insisted it was his space and refused to move but why did the driver not notice him, he was tabby and mainly white and a big cat, this I will never know. He said he just saw a cat run out of the front of the van in a very disorientated manner. He apologised, realising it was a private drive and should not have reversed on it. He sent flowers but that was not enough as he had robbed me of my best friend.

His friend next door was still coming through the cat flap into the house and wondering where he was. I had to close the cat flap and I used to see his friend sitting on the fence waiting and waiting either to come in or for a sight of Brandy coming out of the cat flap. His friends face was often seen in the cat flap window for a about a week and then it ceased. He got the message Brandy was not coming back.

The veterinary fees were huge. It came to £700 and the cremation was £60. Luckily I had Pet Plan insurance which paid for it. He was cremated with his toy whale and his blanket and is now in a little box displayed in the lounge at home.

No other cat will ever replace Brandy but I hope one day I will be able to offer a home to another cat in memory of my beloved pet. Brandy left me so many happy memories that I couldn't and wouldn't want to forget.

Brandy aged 4 on the stairs.

Brandy aged 8 being cheeky - taken the year he was killed.

*Brandy was cremated and he is
home in a little box.*

My Cochlear Implant

I first heard about cochlear implants 23 years ago at the age of 48. My son who was studying medicine at Southampton University had gone along to a lecture given by an ENT surgeon there. He told him that his mother was deaf and he asked him to bring me over and that he would see what he could do. At that time the idea of the "bionic ear" (as the press were wont to call it) was a new one. Initial euphoria was quelled when it was reported that such operations did not allow deaf people to understand speech, for that reason and others cochlear implants have since been given a bad press. The emphasis on speech discrimination means that people tend to forget the other benefits of cochlear implants namely an awareness of environmental sounds, increased confidence through an ability to respond to sound, better speech, some enjoyment of music and relief from tinnitus.

Sound is perceived naturally by way of air and bone conduction.

1. Sound waves travel through the ear canal and strike the eardrum.
2. These sound waves cause the eardrum and the three bones within the middle ear to vibrate.
3. These vibrations are transferred to the fluids in the inner ear – known as the cochlea – and cause the tiny hair cells in the cochlea to move.
4. The movement of the hair cells produces neural impulses which are sent along the hearing nerve to the brain, where they are interpreted as sound.

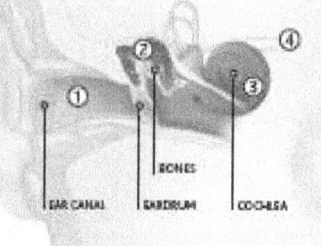

EAR CANAL | EARDRUM | BONES | COCHLEA

ACTUAL SIZE OF THE COCHLEAR

HOW HEARING WORKS - ***NATURAL HEARING***

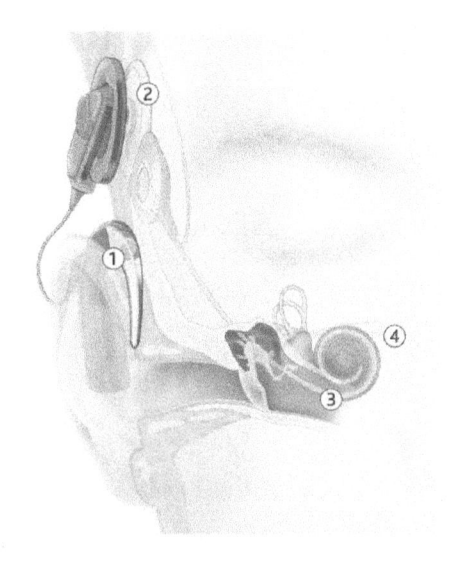

The Nucleus Cochlear Implant bypasses parts of the ear that no longer work properly by sending signals directly to the hearing nerve.

1. Microphones on the sound processor pick up sounds and the processor converts them into digital information.
2. This information is transferred through the coil to the implant just under the skin.
3. The implant sends electrical signals down the electrode into the cochlea.
4. The hearing nerve fibres in the cochlea pick up the signals and send them to the brain, giving the sensation of sound.

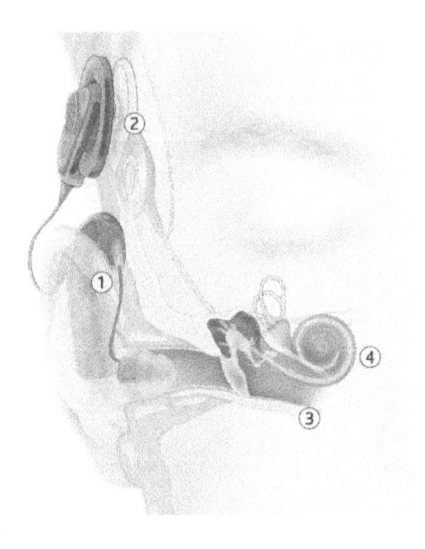

How the acoustic component works

1. The acoustic component, like a hearing aid, amplifies low frequency sounds and sends them via the normal hearing pathway.
2. At the same time, the processor converts high frequency sounds to digital information which is sent to the implant under the skin.
3. The implant sends electrical signals down the electrode into the cochlea, stimulating the nerve fibres.
4. This nerve response is sent to the brain, where it is combined with the response from the amplified sounds from the acoustic component into a perceived sound.

*HOW HEARING WORKS - **WITH A COCHLEAR IMPLANT***

I went over to meet the ENT surgeon, he was apparently a brilliant surgeon and a Dutchman, at Southampton University Institute of Sound and Vibration Research (now known as University of Southampton Auditory Implant Services) and after a series of tests and counselling over six months I was chosen for a cochlear implant.

Southampton University Auditory Implant Services

It wasn't guaranteed how much hearing I would get back, in fact nobody knew. I was one of the first in the U.K. and Jersey to have this implant though they were already being done in America and Australia. I was implanted with the Nucleus 22 channel implant on 29 July 1992. The operation was performed by Mr Norman Haacke. Other designs of cochlear implant have been developed and implanted successfully since. A miracle of precision design and technology, it consists of an electrode array of 22 platinum electrodes attached to a receiver-stimulator package. The arrangement is hermetically sealed in silicone rubber housing. During an operation lasting approximately 3 hours, the electrode array is threaded into the cochlea and the receiver-simulator package is embedded into the bone of the skull, underneath the skin. After a 4 week healing period, the external parts of the implant are now put into action. A directional microphone sits on the ear, sound (speech for example) is transmitted via this microphone to a speech processor. The processor extracts pertinent information about the speech signal, namely the formant (harmonic) frequencies and the spectral energy of the signal. This information is digitised and sent, by electromagnetic induction across the skin, to the receiver-stimulator which activates a number of the electrodes according to what frequencies are required and also according to pre-determined data about the electrode stimulation levels necessary for the particular patient. Ultimately, stimulation of the electrodes activates the acoustic nerve and a sensation of hearing is achieved.

When I was first implanted, the receiver box was the size of a cigarette packet that you clipped on to your clothing or put in your pocket. Things have changed since then and the receiver is now housed in the earpiece itself and sits behind the ear. I have had two upgrades since my first activation. They get smaller and smaller every time and engineers are still working to improve them. Each one that I have had is better than the last, the sounds are more natural.

Although the implant does not restore perfect hearing, the sensation of hearing received through it and the range of frequency it brings to the patient is quite often sufficient for some degree of speech discrimination to be achieved. However, it is important to remember that the crucial part of the process is the two years and more of rehabilitation that follows the implant, mainly hearing therapy - learning to hear all over again, to put meaning to the sounds that are brought by the implant. The importance of this rehabilitation process to the success of the implant is not to be sneezed at, a lot of the time is spent performing countless tests on potential candidates for an implant in order to determine their suitability for the operation. Of the criteria for selection, probably the most important (given medical suitability) is that the expectations of the patient are not excessively high. Having been profoundly deaf since the age of eight I had nothing to lose so once I was offered the implant I had no hesitation in accepting.

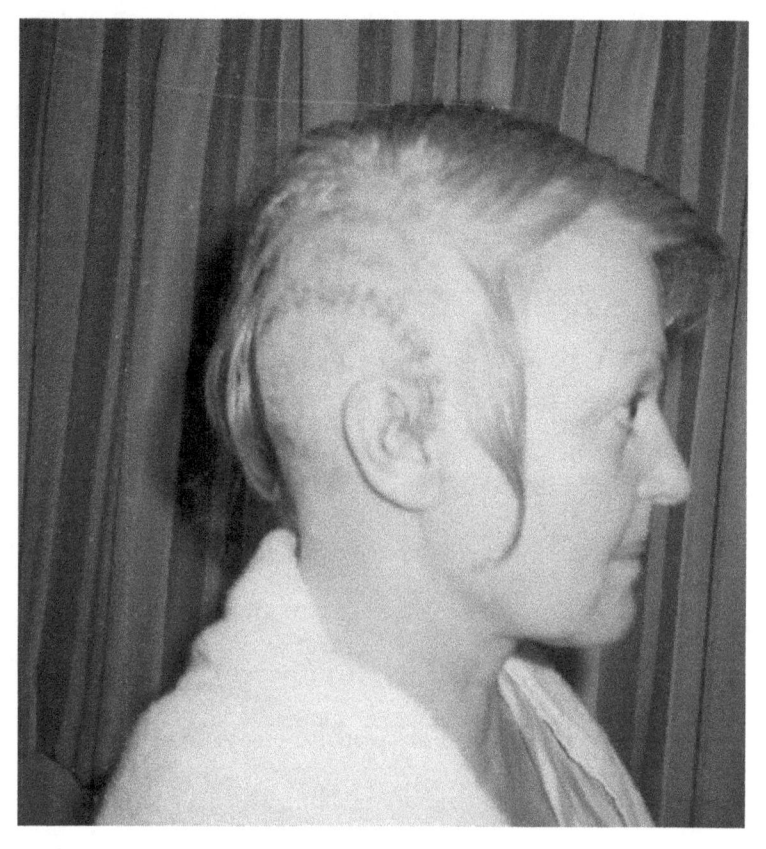

My Cochlear Implant - I had 22 staples on the side of my head - today the incision is a four inch cut behind the ear.

When I returned home after the operation I felt other people's expectations were quite high. It upset me that I couldn't get through to them to explain that my implant does not give perfect hearing or even work some kind of miracle to restore my hearing to what it was. The ignorance of certain people made it very stressful. I have met some very inspiring people with whom I have compared notes on our implants and they have achieved far more than I have which proves that everyone is different to the degree of hearing they achieve from their implants. It also depends on the reason the person lost their hearing and how much hearing that person had before the implant. If I had refused the offer of an implant I would certainly be spending the rest of my life wondering if it would have worked for me.

Four weeks after the implant, which allowed time for the wound to heal, I was switched on. At first all I could hear were a lot of scratchy tinny sounds. Nothing made sense whatsoever. Having been completely deaf since the age of eight, forty years before, my acoustic nerve was extremely rusty and my brain was not primed to cope with this sudden influx of sound. However, continued use of the device brought gradual improvement. I was travelling from my home in Jersey for hearing therapy each month. Together with the dedication and patience of hearing therapists at Southampton University the sounds became clearer. I could hear and recognise sounds in the home such as the washing machine, the fridge humming, the kettle boiling and the door-bell, even the phone ringing. Today I can hear most environmental sounds but speech is very difficult. I can hear the person's voice but cannot tell what they are saying - I still have to lip read. When I was first listening to voices and my therapists were reading passages from a book they sounded like Mickey Mouse and Donald Duck but over the years it became clearer and recognisable as a person's voice. Still I have come a long way from the day I was implanted when I could hear virtually nothing. I was profoundly deaf for a little over forty years before I had my implant. Had they come out when I was in my childhood, who knows, I may hear a lot better today. The length of time from the onset of deafness to my implant may have been too great. Nowadays when a child is born deaf or has become deaf from an illness in their childhood they are implanted within a year or two. This enables the child to grown up with it and learn. I wasn't able to benefit from this as I was in my late forties when I was implanted. I can hear very little and struggle to find what those sounds are.

I once read about a blind man who was three years old when he lost his sight when a bomb exploded when he was playing in his back garden. He was in his 40's when he had surgery to restore his sight. Soon after he wrote his story which highlighted an example for me in describing my deafness. He could see but when asked to describe the colours on a chart on the wall he could not tell you what the colours were. He was three years old when he was blinded and had no memory of colours and couldn't tell you if they were blue or red, green or yellow. He had to learn all over again. I thought it gave a very good example of how I am learning to hear.

My Cochlear Implant has given me a lot of awareness of sound and I can identify some of them. I have been told that this is about all I will ever achieve. Sadly it hasn't changed my life as I had hoped. However disappointing it may be, I couldn't hear a sound for forty years so what I hear today is something better than silence.